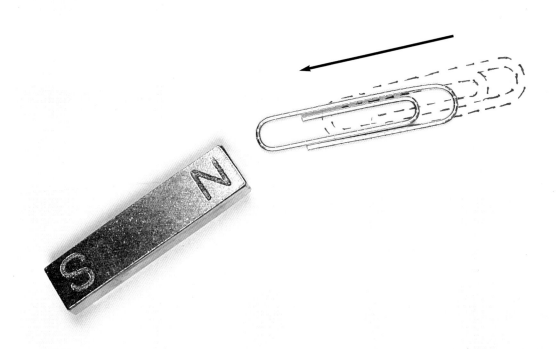

Magnets make things move
without touching them.

Most magnets are **metal.**

Magnets can make other
pieces of metal move.

Magnets pull things towards them.

Magnets can also push
things away from them.

Magnets can move
paper clips.

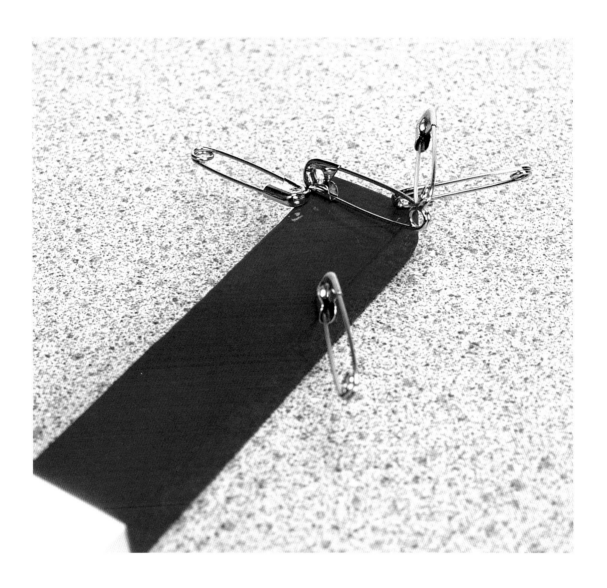

Magnets can move
safety pins.

Magnets cannot move wood.

Magnets cannot move **plastic.**

Magnets help us to build things.

Magnets hold paper up
on fridges.

Magnets help to open cans.

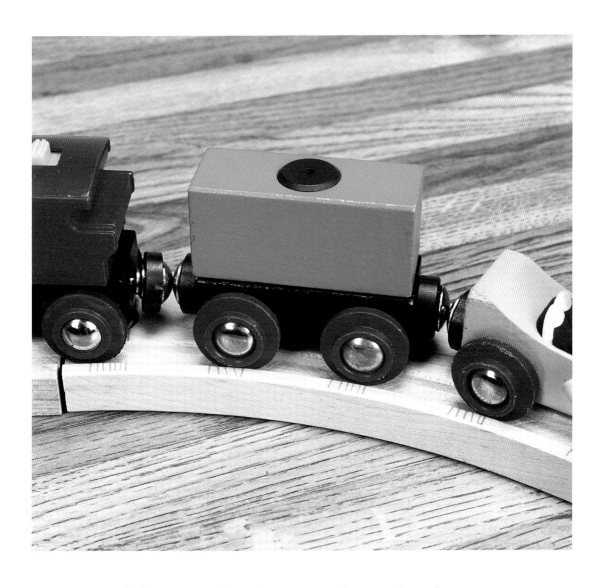

Magnets keep toy trains together.

Magnets help to show us
the way to go.

Magnets are everywhere.

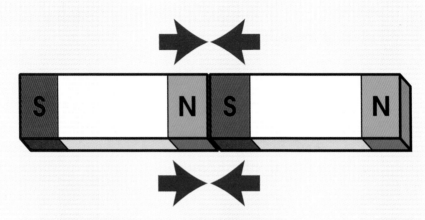

DIFFERENT poles PULL together.

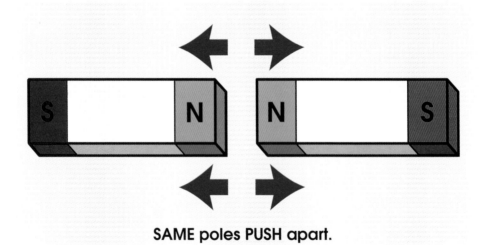

SAME poles PUSH apart.

18

Poles

Every magnet has two ends. One end is called the north pole. The other end is called the south pole.

Look at the top picture. The different poles pull towards each other. The north pole (N) of one magnet pulls the south pole (S) of another magnet towards it.

Look at the bottom picture. Two north poles are pushing apart. This is because the same poles push away from each other.

Magnet Facts

 Magnets can only move things that are made out of certain metals, such as iron and steel.

 A magnet is strongest at each of its ends.

 A magnet can be made in any shape. Most magnets are shaped like horseshoes or bars.

The Earth is actually a giant magnet.

 The needle in a compass is a magnet. The needle always points north.

 A rock called a lodestone is a natural magnet. Lodestones are made out of a mineral called magnetite.

Glossary

 magnets – metal that iron sticks to

 metal – something that many things are made of. Metal is usually shiny and hard. Metal comes from the ground.

 plastic – something that lots of things are made of. Plastic can be any colour or shape. Plastic is made by people.

The photographs in this book are reproduced through the courtesy of: © Todd Strand/Independent Picture Service, cover, pp. 2, 3, 4, 5, 6, 7, 8, 9, 10, 11, 12, 13, 14, 15, 22 (all); © Roger Ressmeyer/CORBIS, p. 16; Digital Vision Royalty Free, p. 17.

Illustration on p. 18 by Laura Westlund.

This book was first published in the United States of America in 2004.

First published in the United Kingdom in 2008 by
Lerner Books,
Dalton House,
60 Windsor Avenue,
London SW19 2RR

Website addess: www.lernerbooks.co.uk

This edition was updated and edited for UK publication by Discovery Books Ltd.,
Unit 3, 37 Watling Street, Leintwardine, Shropshire SY7 0LW

Words in **bold** are explained in the glossary on page 22.

British Library Cataloguing in Publication Data

Nelson, Robin, 1971-
Magnets. - (First step nonfiction. Forces)
1. Magnets - Juvenile literature 2. Magnetism - Juvenile
literature
I. Title
538.4

ISBN-13: 978 1 58013 368 5

Printed in China

Index